C000119976

I Married
the Angel
of the North

To Doreen

With best

wishes

Pete P

ALSO BY PETER MORTIMER

Stage Plays
Snow White in the Black Lagoon
The Troutbeck Time Traveller
The Man Who Played with Mice
Imagine
IT
Elvis, Lucy & Capt. Sensible
Doris Dumpling & The Magic Corner Shop
Dunce, Crafty & The Great Monster Robbery
The Enchanted Pudding
Spirits of the Deep
Whiter than Wight
A Change in the Weather
The Trip
Arthur Raises the Roof
The Nightwatchman
Making Plans for Winkle
Clockman
Lower the Lake!

Poetry
A Rainbow in its Throat
(The Expanded) Utter Nonsense

Real Life
The Last of the Hunters
Broke Through Britain
100 Days on Holy Island

Fable/Fiction
The Witch & the Maiden
Croak, the King & a Change in the Weather

I Married the Angel of the North

Peter Mortimer

Five Leaves Publications

www.fiveleaves.co.uk

I Married the Angel of the North

Peter Mortimer

Published in 2002 by
Five Leaves Publications,
PO Box 81, Nottingham
NG5 4ER, UK
www.fiveleaves.co.uk

Five Leaves acknowledge financial support
from East Midlands Arts

east **midlands**
arts
making creative
opportunities

ISBN 0 907123 93 7

Acknowledgments are due to the editors of the following
publications in which some of these poems first appeared:
*Acumen, Blade, Broke Through Britain, Chapman, Life
Lines Review, The Golden Girl Anthology, Headlock, Honest
Ulsterman, IRON, The North, Odyssey, Other Poetry,
Pigeonhole, Poetry Durham*

Design and layout by Four Sheets Design and Print Ltd
Printed in Great Britain

Contents

I MARRIED THE ANGEL OF THE NORTH

I married the Angel of the North.
I led it down no church aisle
no church aisle could contain it.
There was no top hat or rice
no tin cans rattling after honeymoon cars
no cutting a three-tiered cake.
But I said to the Angel, "I do"
and the Angel said "I do", too.
I kissed it lightly though it has no lips
I put an arm round a small part
of its rusting legs. I ran my finger
down its ribbed feet.
I know the Angel can't embrace me
can't wrap those flattened wings around me
can't move its muscular legs to clasp me.
I know its sexual organs don't really exist
and I can't tell if it has breasts.
I know it can't spend all day with me
mooning and spooning and making daisy chains.
I know it can't stand on the cruise ship deck
under a hanging lantern moon, and whisper
this moment should last forever.
I know the Angel lives on its small hilltop.
I know I can never own the Angel
but I love the Angel of the North
and have married it.
Because this is a marriage that can last
and the Angel will never leave me.
Other people may marry the Angel as well.
This causes me no problems.

I stand by the Angel of the North
hear its wings sing the wind.
The Angel knows nothing of the old songs
its face turned away from memory.
Its metal head holds no images
of cloth caps, mufflers, dolly tubs,
the dark choking pit
or men welded to a tanker's hull.

I have married the Angel of the North
because it is bigger than me
because its roots are 100ft deep in northern soil
because it is always in when I call
because it is always in flight when I call
because it sees horizons the rest of us don't
because in my waking dreams
the imagined wush-wushing
of those great boat-paddle wings
pushes the slowing blood
through all our northern veins.

FIVE PLACES IT MIGHT HAPPEN

1. On the Escalator

You stagger slightly, clutching a copy
of that day's newspaper. The woman behind you,
going home to newly planted petunias
takes you for a drunk
as you stumble against her.
Then your legs go. Then everything.

2. In the Cinema

Some forgotten matinee, the click
of the final curtain, the quick creak
of sprung-back seats as the audience
drifts away from the unread credits.
The usherette, whose 10 day diet is not working,
swishes her torch along the rows
of discarded popcorn and scrunched wrappers
where you are still sitting.

3. In the Department Store

Passing the perfumed quiet of the cosmetics counters
your heart clenches to a fist. You reach out,
blindly scatter the tasteful display of *Chanel*.
You fall. Above you, faces hover like moons.
The assistant with the perfect skin cries:
"Stand back — some air!"

4. On a Crowded Bus

Downstairs, next to a 40 year old insurance clerk
who smells of stale smoke and suspects
his wife of an affair. He notices nothing.
Your single gasp goes unheard
by the young mother in front
shaking a tired rattle at the bawling baby.
Here's the conductor, his hand lightly
on your shoulder. "Fares please."

5. In the Bosom of Your Own Home

You are propped up on plump pillows.
The doctor, who's considering private practice
clicks shut the black case
offers hushed words downstairs.
You are clinging on.
After setting video recorders, oven controls
or answerphones, relatives visit.
They are like guests too early for the party.
What can they do?
They sit round your bed
dab an eye, shuffle their feet
notice a badly tied lace
or the increased weight of cousin Tony.

ADVICE TO A WRITER

Read everything you can
Remember it all
Forget it all
Avoid philosophers, politicians
and professors of English Literature
Prepare for poverty
Spend a lot of time alone
Spend a lot of time in noisy rabbles
Listen to criticism as much as praise
Remember critics would rather be writing a poem
Don't spend more than one year in a writers' circle
Invest in a large waste paper basket
Place your desk away from the window
Imagine everything
Never retire
Remember, the writing is more important than the writer
Don't advertise toothpaste or anything else
Go out in the worst kinds of weather
Live at least once on a small island
Lose yourself in a large city
Be nosey
Weep for the stupidity of humanity
Laugh loudly at the same stupidity
Only write true
Learn to know when you don't
(headache, sleeplessness, bad temper etc)
Learn to know when you do
(sleeplessness, headache etc)
Be absurd about the serious
treat seriously the absurd
Echo every writer that has ever lived
Write like nobody else
Occasionally sit at your desk in midnight's silence
and do nothing at all
Realise your writing changes nothing and is essential
Be at the centre of everything

Be at the edge and invisible
Never run out of teabags
Do one more draft
Remember, easy writing makes bad reading
Good writing outlives the writer
Bad writing doesn't live at all
Beware reactions from friends and family
Write more. Then write less
Avoid all literary theory
Dance and sing every day. Alone if necessary
Let one half of you be calm
Let the other half be restless
Feel naked without a notebook
Spend an inordinate amount of time
Observing a slug or some such
See what no-one else has seen
Even in a rusty nail, or a damp cloth.

MR PESQUOD AND THE RAIN

People are running from the deluge
hunched up, headless.
People are pressing themselves
like dried flowers
under gutters and in doorways.

Rain tap-dances on cars
skateboards down roof tiles
shimmies towards drains.
On the greasy street
the puddle's rainbow streak
is splintered by running feet.

Mr Pesquod is still.
His arms are spread wide
his head tilted back
his eyes closed.

The saturation of his shirt
advertises his pale chest.
His skin has turned liquid
his hair molten
his shoes are inaccessible islands.
His upturned spectacles
starburst with water.
His pockets are filling up.

High in the sky, word has got out.
The falling rain drops twist and turn
trying every trick they know
to land on the increasingly liquid
Mr Pesquod.

BEIGE

Beige has nothing to say.
Beige does not know how to sing
it cannot move to the rhythms of music.
Beige cannot muster an orgasm
to make the moon tremble.
Climbing a tree to shout
from the highest branch, is an idea
that never enters beige's head.
Even one thousand people
appearing over a hilltop
seem rather ordinary
if dressed in beige.

When you suspect someone of wearing beige
check it out. If there is no heartbeat
that is beige
if the pulse is cold and still
that is beige.
You may discover such people
carefully organising their lives
in supermarkets, DIY centres,
car showrooms, building society offices.
Say to them "don't be afraid",
though beige is always afraid.

The older these people are
the more beige must be discouraged.
The young may survive beige
but the old are slowly consumed;
It works its quiet way up
through shoes socks trousers,
skirts, cardigans, shirts and jackets
till that unchallenged moment of death
when beige paints its wasted pallor
across those acres of silent skin.

CANCER
(*for Sally Walker*)

They cut something from you
pressed the sharp steel to your flesh
sliced as neatly as a butcher
incising sirloin steaks.
They circled the target in marker paint
cut away, tossed it into the blue plastic
removing this thing from its only known home

How could it know it had rocked
and wrecked our century
its appetite shrivelling its million victims
to husks, turning them hairless
turning their skin to dried parchment?
How could it know our fear of its name
that not even shocko stand-ups use in jest?

You never saw it, it moved where you moved
to the corner shop, through busy streets
the motorway's length. But moved also
when you were still, tiny terrible movements
reasons unknown, closing on this cell
that cell, and feeding
with no more thought than we consume
the multiplex popcorn, the sealed foil takeaway.

And in a thousand bleached hospitals
under cool white lights
patients are slabbed out on tables
robed figures cut, cut, metal to flesh
as iron age hunters cut, metal to flesh.

9

Your enemy announced itself, pushed its small hump
under the skin you inspected daily
the skin your lover's touch caressed.
A lump, a bump, a declaration of real war
not some jumped-up conflict
over meaningless boundaries
nor some greedy grabbing for mineral rights
not some crazed ambition of a would-be omnipotent
but here in your breast, a civil war, eating its silent way
through our progress, our civilisation
our enlightenment.

And how do we know when this thing is killed?
Like some hallowe'en Jason, some Terminator
some Frankenstein's monster, its bludgeoned body
lies inert, then rises again, begins again.
How do we, this species that destroys everything
destroy it? How do we, experts at annihilation
wipe it out?

This blip on the screen, this smudge on the X-ray
that lives in the dark, the silence, the isolation.
It tolls our funeral bells, it leaves empty chairs
at our dinner tables, suits hanging unused
in wardrobes. It causes our children
to turn in doomed hope at every click of the gate.
It leaves us abandoned in our fitted kitchens
our centrally heated homes
in front of our flickering screens.

What powers it? What is it for?
Why does it make its murderous home
in the bodies of our tortured species
while elsewhere, the planet's cells remain unstained?

HOOK A DUCK

After answering the questions
contestants are invited to hook a duck.
They pass the duck (hooked) to Zelda
who unscrews its bottom. Inside
is a small card which she passes to Larry.
The card states the contestant's prize.
This could be two weeks in Tenerife
a hover-mower, kitchen units
a four ring eye level grill gas cooker
or a stale carrot!

In which year was the St.Valentine's Day Massacre?

A drum roll precedes Larry's announcement.
He likes to raise his eyebrows, tug his spotted bow tie
dig the contestants in the ribs.
The studio audience is pumped up;
they cheer and whistle at the big prizes.
For the likes of the carrot
they let out a long "aaaaaaah!"

How many teams have won the Cup & League double?

The contestants go first to make-up
faces dabbed like babies' bottoms.
One glass of wine in hospitality. More later.
Leandre's from Bolton. Spent two hours
under the drier
twenty minutes in front of the mirror.
Half of Bromsgrove would be watching for Louise
Eight years at that chicken factory.
Only her boyfriend knows her secret;
on telly with no knickers!
Arthur's good on history. Wars of the Roses?
A doddle. His wife bought the shirt. From Accrington.
Gusset. That's the word Wayne's mates have bet
he can't get into an answer. Five pints on it.

Who wrote the Sherlock Holmes novels?

Sometimes Zelda's fishnet tights go right up her arse.
Once in the Bizzy Buzzer spot, she came on.
Luckily the show's recorded. That bloke from Ipswich —
three takes to film his spontaneous surprise
at winning the stereo. Couldn't get it right.

Which is the stronger, a gale or a hurricane?

Sometimes Zelda wished she had more to do.
She leads the contestants onstage.
"This is Patricia from Oswestry. Patricia's a housewife."
She unscrews the duck's bottom. She leads them off.
That's it. Still. Loads of people envy her
stop her in the street. Autographs.
She's opened six supermarkets.

What was the surname of Sonny and Cher?

And Larry. Thrusting into her
in those hotel rooms. She liked to watch
his face when he came. Close up
you saw the lines. Millions knew that face.
Knew his catch-phrase: *MUSTN'T GRUMBLE!*
She'd met his wife once. A bit overweight.
The truth was, sex with Larry didn't bother her
one way or the other.

Who said, I have nothing to declare but my genius?

A year's waiting list for contestants.
The audience loved it. Deep in that sound-proof studio
the rest of the world shut out.
Hot lights, warm up, camera-man
theme tune, flashing staircase
and tripping down it came Larry
like some bloody messiah thought Zelda.
They clapped and clapped
Sometimes, she thought
if the floor manager asked them
they'd clap forever.

Is the Antarctic the North or the South pole?

They didn't want to leave, to go back
to mortgages, damp patches, surly kids
insurance premiums, the bastards next door,
the spouse, that dodgy hoover.
Clapped and clapped. And her and Larry
smiling, bowing, as the credits rolled
waving goodbye. And Larry's little trick
his unseen hand, tweaking her arse.
And Larry's little joke, bowing and smiling
and between the clenched teeth of his smile
at the music's big finale, lips hardly moving
just loud enough for her:
"Now fuck off home, the lot of you".

BLOOD DONOR

This could be the morgue
or any hospital
or some hall, arranged post-disaster.
The face-up bodies lie silent
while their blood drains peacefully away.
And in each squeezed fist
a rubber stick is slowly turned.

On one bare arm, the needle
has pierced the heart
of a rampant dragon.
The man wears t-shirt, jeans;
each chew of his gum motors slightly
the sluggish liquid.

But what if they just kept going
left his sump open
replaced each filled bottle
with another, till the slow
pulsing spurts became drips
then nothing, his veins
like sucked out straws?

He can hear the chink of tea cups
the soft footfall of nurses
The unhooking of donors' charts.
He has the ceiling's cork pattern
to study. On the next bed
a woman seems as close as a lover.

Soon his blood will invade another
will swirl to a new identity
part of him will swim silently
in the sunless veins of a stranger;
a petty thief maybe, rock star, wages clerk,
bus driver, child molester, ballet dancer.
His blood will have no argument
will follow the required route
will flood its new heart
as easily as the old.

He feels dreamy. His turned head
squeaks the pillow's plastic.
He sees, in the hall's far corner
a white-coated woman stabbing thumbs.
Dabs of cotton wool turn florid.

Days later, the anger.
Who could have started it?
Closing time, the car park of Sinatras
a car quickly reversed, smashed headlight.
Twat! Fuck you! Ye what? I said, fuck you!
His fist thuds into the driver's face
and the blood that flowers on his knuckles
is the blood of another
and the blood of himself.

THE P.R. EXEC. INTRODUCES POTENTIAL CLIENTS TO *THE MATURITY PROGRAMME PACKAGE*

Ladies and gentlemen, on behalf of Vent Brockway Ltd.
let me welcome you to today's presentation.
My name is Nigel, one of the firm's senior consultants.
By now you should have our colour-coded
Information package, handed out by my colleague Denise.
Thank you Denise.
Allow me, if you will, to guide you through it.
There will be time for questions
after which we can talk informally
over the finger buffet and wine

Section one (Everglade Green) concerns skin changes.
You will be aware of what we call *The Wrinkle Bonus.*
Over the years your skin develops interesting lines
contours and creases. How different from your youth —
that flat featureless skin, which we call
The Lincolnshire Syndrome. A flat landscape
ladies and gentlemen, is a boring landscape.

On to Section Two (Heliotrope) our scientifically
programmed aural and visual redefinitions.
We call this *Happiness through Diminution.*
Imagine how many daily distressing sounds and images
we are forced to endure. Suffering. Pain. Imagine you
were able slowly to filter them out via a reduction
in your aural and visual intake.
As the poet might have put it
Who wants to hear and see/So much misery?
You won't have to.

If you move to Section Three (Crocus Yellow)
You'll find what we call *Limb Dignity.*
Look around you Ladies and Gentlemen
note how our modern world rushes pell-mell
yet never seems to get anywhere. Note the stress levels
of modern life. We aim to reduce those levels.
As your limbs slow down, as an unnecessary sense
of urgency dies away, your new pace will give time
to take in your surroundings.

Could we move on to Section Four (Coral Reef Blue),
The Memory Lapse Agenda. As you mature
we guarantee those sweet memories of youth
will grow ever more vivid. The more mundane memory,
what you did yesterday, those hours spent
dribbling into a tartan rug, the slow tortuous
journeys on your Zimmer etc; these will simply
be forgotten, or blurred.

I mention memory, which brings me to Section Five
(Scent of Lilac). How many of us remember the horrors
of toothache? That throbbing insistent pain?
All of us! Here at Vent Brockway we have a phrase:
No tooth, no toothache, a phrase which perfectly defines
The Molar Reduction Programme
specifically designed for your greater pleasure.

And finally (Mollusc Pink). We call this *Vestment Vision,*
an opportunity to eliminate that annoying decision,
that sense of frustration felt by us all.
You stand before the mirror. What clothes required
for this wedding, for that party, for that holiday?

You simply cannot decide! Be *Sage in Beige*
Eliminate all such needless decisions.
Increasingly you will find yourself merging
becoming part of the greater whole
the isolation of individual identity removed.

You will have *Happiness through Diminution*
You will have the *Wrinkle Bonus*
You will have *Limb Dignity*
You will be strengthened by *Memory Lapse Agenda*
You will benefit from *Molar Reduction Programme*
And last, you will be *Sage in Beige*

Thank you. I'm happy to take those questions now.

SNOW

The world is shushed by snow,
made silent; dark secrets
gagged with brilliant white,
What was ugly is no longer so.

At the first touch of flakes
people hunch themselves homewards
turn collars against the weightless fall
hurry to the sanctuary of radiators.

On tufted *Welcome* mats
they stamp off the clinging white,
or indoors, brush it from coats
as it turns to twinkling diamonds
in the steady heat.

They sweep it from paths
sting it with sprinkled salt
toss it from scraped shovels
to form cancerous mounds.
It's pushed rudely aside
by the snow-plough's jutting shield,
left to a dirty roadside death
of splashed mud
and the drunkard's patterned piss.

When snow first falls
open your palm, allow
one silent flake to fall
watch how simply it dies
how it turns to an unwept tear
in your unclenched fist.

MR. PARKIN'S AUTUMN

Having struggled briefly from its bed
the sun yawns, and is sinking back.
Gathered by the wind
a posse of dead leaves rides out of town.
By the cul-de-sac bottom
the garaged *Mr. Tastee* van
stares blinkless at the brick wall
and waits for the Spring raspberry ripple
to fill its bellies.

At no.12, Mr. Parkin waits for tomorrow
thinking of that shed bench
where he'll scatter the silver-fish nails
from the grimy glass jar, fix for good
that flipping cat flap. He'll glug the mucus
anti-freeze down the throat of his green Fiesta
for its occasional Safeway journey.
He'll grease those stiff secateurs
as once he greased his black thatch
for tea dance afternoons with Thelma.

As every year, he'll watch the hedge die
and be slowly busy till dusk
till he sets that table for two
curling the red napkins to standing cones
as neat, as erect as fifty years ago;
a young waiter in Torquay.

Over the cottage pie, Mr. Parkin's question:
"Thelma, which one of us this year
will spot the last maple leaf?"
and the serviette opposite will slightly
droop its head in response.

CARRIED ON THE WIND

1. Suburban

The metallic chimes of the ice-cream van
the wish-swish of the neighbour's
shimmying sprinkler. The distant drone
of some aircraft, chalking the blue.
The twittering of bird bath starlings
The efficient clip-clip of the crew-cutting shears.

2. Elsewhere

The shriek of the mountaineer
whose misplaced foot slides him to oblivion.
The cry of the capsized sailor
gently rocking in a sea about to swallow her.
The doomed gasp of those clutching
the heart's final stab.

3. Also Elsewhere

The crunch of human bones
beneath the tank's trundling track
the scream of the torture victim
whose finger nails sulphorously flare.
The shriek of the villagers
hacked away by soldiers
for a cause partially understood.
The silence of refugees
shuffling a ragged line
to another unwelcome place.

4. Suburban (again)

The wind ruffles the hair of Barbara
reclined on her sun lounger.
As she bites her bottom lip
to a bead of blood, the wind
carries from the patio doors
the sound of Donald, smashing to bits
the reluctant lumps of ice.

FAMOUS PEOPLE & UNFAMOUS PEOPLE

Unfamous people don't understand
when famous people attempt suicide.
Unfamous people suspect being famous is a better bet
than being unfamous.
Being featured in the media
owning large secluded properties
travelling the world, mixing with the glamorous
being recognised in the street, photographed
at airports and in restaurants;
why would such people (think unfamous people)
want to slash their wrists?

Unfamous people seem to think being paid large sums
for acting in films, playing in the Premier League
or modelling clothes round the world, must be better
than being paid small sums for putting jam into tarts
selling fruit & veg, stitching jeans in a factory
or catching fish in an icy sea.

Unfamous people are hopeless
at understanding the pressures of the famous.
Which is probably why, though famous people
(suicidal or not), rely on unfamous people
for their livelihood, they would prefer
in the main, not to be with them.

WINDOW CLEANER

Each working day he creates
new triangles, one for every house he visits.
He climbs the triangle's longest side
like a monkey. At the top he goes to work.
His bucket hangs from the rusty nail
like an earring. Beneath him, within a frame of air
he has defined a three-sided picture.

His work done, he climbs down.
Like a parade ground soldier
he swings his ladder to his shoulder
and walks on. The air leaks back
to formlessness. The triangle forgets itself.
More pictures are waiting, more defining
he'll think nothing of.

SILENCE

simply waits
for all sound to cease.
The baby's laughter
the roar of Niagara
a nuclear combustion
the beat of a drum.
When they are exhausted
silence will step in.

Silence can not be exhausted.
Listen — more sounds
are jostling for position;
the motorway's thrum
the junky's dark scream
the cabaret applause
ice cubes in gin.

Silence is patient.
Its time will come.
Dumbly acknowledged
and lasting forever

MAN FALLS FROM 18th STOREY WINDOW
(The film is run slow)

He floats down like a feather.
Like a snowflake. He could have time
to adjust his tie, pull up his socks
arrange his hair for a soft landing.
He does none of these things.
His body turns as slow as a barbecue chicken.

He would have time to stare
into each passing window;
the clerk with the two hour cigarette
The touch-typist at 15 *wpm*
the tea-bag, dunked for a full hour.

By storey ten, he's horizontal,
A falling pencil. Storey eight
and he's tilting, head first
arms stretched down as if
planning some hand-stand finale
when the ground rises to meet him.

Storey six and he's on his back.
He could be a swimmer, or a rocked baby.
He could be dreaming in a hammock.
Four storeys from earth
he raises his right arm, as if
in supplication. He's nearly done.
His rippled suit jacket tugs
at its one fastened button.
Here comes the pavement
First, it's his head.
It bounces slowly, once, twice
like a tennis ball on a casually
carried racket. Then his body.
On first contact it seems tossed
gently — a lettuce leaf in a colander,
The limbs, movement all comic;
Like some daft clown
like some boasting body-popper
like that double-jointed show-off
we remember from school.

Then the body's still and stays still.
No matter what speed we run on the film
No matter how fast or slow we make
the gathering crowd.

READ A BOOK EVERY DAY

Yes, read a book every day!
Even when other matters intrude
a row in the family
an interview for a job
the garage door that needs painting
a pulled calf muscle —
still find time for that book!
If a close friend happens by
at the wrong time, shout
from an upstairs window: "Sorry —
the book!" If the weather forecast
warns of flash floods, retire
to the highest part of the house
with water wings and the book.
There may be a general election
Friends may be flocking to see
a famous actor open a new sushi restaurant.
A demolition gang may be moving in up the street.
Don't let this put you off. Rumours could be rife
of giant ants three miles away
devouring everything in their path
or a strange spectral mist moving in your direction
turning people into plantpots.
This is the time to keep faith in your book.
Sometimes a book is unusually helpful
in dealing with strange spectral mists.
The worst thing is not to be protected by any book.
It's worse than being tossed naked
onto a bed of sharp nails
or being trapped in a field of angry bulls
wearing a bright red poppy suit
worse than being 20,000 feet up in a hang glider
with no wings. Worse than lining up
for the 100 metres Olympics final
and finding you've only one leg

or falling into an active volcano
with a rucksack of TNT strapped to your back.
Worse than being in a broken-down lift
with a sloth.

Lots of people don't read a book every day.
When they learn the truth, it's too late.
They go through life thinking a book
is just paper and ink, something from a shop
like nasal decongestant, cushioned insoles
dental fixative, or a musical birthday cake
that slowly revolves.

These people will say to you
"Why bother reading a book?"
"What difference does a book make?"
And hey, look! Here comes that strange spectral mist
that turns people into plantpots
and these bookless people not knowing
how to handle it at all.

THREE HAIKU

On the corpse's head
hair alive
to the wind

Hearse on cobblestones;
the clattering
of false teeth

The drunk's embrace;
the lamp-post remains
stiff-backed

THE SEA'S LOST LOVER

Where has he gone
who loved her so long
before stars blinked open their eyes?
When the earth's molten heart
was still bubbling and strong
and no bird wings
brush-stroked the skies.

She cannot forget
nor lie still like a lake
that's spread, open-legged to the sky.
Her searching is soaked
into rocks, into cliffs
which brush her away, like a fly.

Twice every day,
humped swollen, and grey
driven in to the frayed edge of land
her searching dissolves
into flowers of foam
hissing back from the shingle and sand.

Luxury liners
lone week-end sailors
are glued to her heaving despair.
With a shrug of her shoulders
she can swallow them whole.
Where is her lover, oh where?

MARRIAGE

She asks him;
what's that troubled look?
Nothing.
And what's that beating
softly in your chest?
Nothing. Nothing. Nothing.

STREET THEATRE MAN

He knows he'll return home later
to a cold bed, the half-emptied wardrobe
the short note still propped on the table.

But still he jiggles his sticks
and flicks the diabolo so high
(to the *ooohs* and the *aaahs* of the crowd)
that it seems for just those few seconds
it will spin and spin ever upward
will escape those forces that chain it
to the unrelenting earth.

LATER

After the dark's donned its suit
and the settee's crouched in shadow.
After the radiator's ticked cold
and the cocoa dregs dried to crust.
After the fire's slumped to grey
and the street lights are off-duty.
After you've read your ten pages
and the clock digits blink unnoticed.
After mumbling yourself to sleep
with the mattress finally exhaled:

Hydrangeas poke heads through the curtains
the fridge milk burps a white bubble
the bath plug spins on its end
the video records its own heartbeat
the kettle light flashes morse code
cushions breathe in and breathe out
the wallpaper adjusts its position
the minah bird swallows its cage
the carpet spreads out on the ceiling
the front door yawns itself open
the cutlery forms into sculptures
the coat stand picks a few pockets.

In the morning you wake from oblivion
and over the crunching of cornflakes
examine your preference share fortunes
in *The Mail* propped up on the ketchup
that's still not totally resettled
from a night-time of cartwheel exertions.

MRS. SPRATT

Eat lean? That's a joke.
Jack scoffs the lot
leaves me those gristly bits
like congealed snot. I mean,
who eats fat by choice?

I watch him sharpen the knife
snick-snack, crossed swords.
Beef, pork, lamb, all
carved as thin as stamp hinges.
The tender curves fall to the plate.
They're his. Mine's the fat.

"There now, my love! Fat
just how you like it!"

Maybe he believes it.
Who can remember when it started?
Swallowing is like some Sumo wrestler
forced down the throat.

People think we're wonderful
a balanced couple. Lean and fat
yin and yang. Jack smiles to hear them
it means as much to him
as his *TESSA* bonds, his electricity shares
his golf club committee.
"Teamwork!" he beams to his friends
and his arm clamps round me.
You could say it keeps us together.

One dinner party I rose slowly
smoothed down my little black number
and with a dab to the lips
whispered, "excuse me".
The mangled gristle heaved its way
up my throat, splashed down
into the toilet bowl's scented blue.
Two flushes, a squidge of toothpaste
some quick mascara, and no-one knew.

I should have spoken up years ago;
now the truth's too hard to swallow.
At night I trace fatty patterns
on the ceiling, feel Jack's pushy thing
inside me, and think of those chump chop lumps
that I chew and chew and chew.

PROSPECTS

One evening, as the same bus
took him from the same office
through the same city streets
to the same house
a rainbow curved down
to print a small fierce mark
on his faded suit jacket.

Only later were its brilliant colours
noticed, and then
by his bright-eyed lover
who at that time
he still had to meet.

IF LOVE
(For Kitty)

If love was cloud
we would eat it from fairground sticks
if love was darkness
we would fill our black pots with its paint
if love was the sun
we would pin it to our lapels
if love was the moon
we would pick our teeth with its crescent
if love was sand
we would build our dreams in its castles
if love was fire
we would flap its red silk at the dead
if love was a tree
we would know its reason for pointing
if love was water
we would frame it into mirrors
if love was rock
we would sink inside its clenched muscle
if love was colour
we would slide down its rainbow back
if love was death, was death
we would tilt its black hat, and kiss
its bone lips into singing

I DREAM OF US ASLEEP

The day's turmoil is stilled
and I dream of us asleep.

While the milkman's note uncurls in its bottle
while the fire's last embers slump unnoticed
while the digital clock blinks its next number.

While buses are silent in their garage
while skin forms on the nightwatchman's tea
and in the city's untrodden puddles
the wrinkled fruit gum reflections
of the traffic lights change unseen.

I dream of us asleep
our limbs are trees' tangled roots
our mouths breathe secrets to each other
our veins criss-cross in their pulsing
our shuttered eyes quiver.
Beyond the world, we know everything
know stillness, know silence
know we are together, and alone.

Come the dawn, we must yank the sun
from its bed, hurry it on its way
to warm the crumbling ruin
to warm the greenest shoot.

We have dipped our hands to its core
we are scorched, we are on fire
with flames that will not sleep.

FORWARD

Condemned to drag ourselves
forward, ever slower

longing to go back
to those places
of no return.

BELIEVE IT

Before you were born
nothing happened
when you are dead
nothing will happen.

HEIR

His future laid out
like the butler's
careful arrangement
of suits.

NEW MUSIC

He woke to the downstairs smell of bacon
the raking of the front room fire.
Soon there would be his father's bathroom gargle
a kitchen chair scraped to proper position
the banging down of the shaken HP.

This Sunday, through the wedged window, a new noise
squeezing its way between cramped roofs.
He listened, then quickly dressed, took the stairs
in threes, a passing raised hand to his mother
as she baptised the chuckling egg.
Her shout followed him from the door:
"Breakfast in two minutes!"

Something about them frightened him
the stiff red and black uniforms
the set-faced trumpeters, cheeks blown
to hard apples. The big belly of the drum
its sound gagged by the cloth stick;
the tambourine players, sad-faced women in glasses
flat shoes and pinned hair. The overweight bassoon
held like a dancing partner, its cold spine
fingered by a man with bitten-down nails.
The red neck of the conductor, his baton waved
like a crab's claw.

After three tunes, the silence.
Their bodies slackened, someone coughed
they fiddled about, prepared to move off,
to another empty street.
A trumpeter banged spit from his mouthpiece
another laid down his instrument like a baby.
The drummer lifted his stiff cap
and dabbed the grey lettuce of his hanky
to the glistening pink brow.

From the blond girl at the back
flashed the glint of a silver triangle.
As she turned, the wind caught her black skirt
curled its corner above the regulation stocking.
That strip of white flesh; his groin quickened
that same unspoken feeling he'd known
at the top of the gymnasium rope.
And what rubbed against his thigh
pulsed stronger than his heart.

At home the glutinous HP collar
was staining his dad's *Sunday People*.
His mother clattered at the sink
waiting to chastise him
and shove him the dried-up egg.

WHAT MOTHER TOLD ME

Look before you leap
it's a long road that has no tulips
a stitch in time saves nine
every cloud has a silver fish
still waters run deep
a limping man has no accent
travel broadens the mind
practise what you eat
there's no smoke without fire
tall trees see the cavalry first
more hands make less work
a basted turkey knows the time of day
blood is thicker than water
the smaller the dog, the fiercer the wee-wee
it's always darkest before the dawn
love is blind drunk
an apple a day keeps the doctor away
a toothless woman can still dance with a bear
more haste, less speed
a crumpled hat holds many eggs
pride comes before a fall
let sleeping dogs, if they want to
it takes a worried man to sing a worried song
the longest journey starts with a cheeseburger
the devil makes work for idle hands
like father like chocolate
a fool and his mummy
live now pay later
he who laughs last is called Norman
never judge a book by its contents
too many Cooks, not enough Entwhistles.

FIVE CHANNEL TUNNEL HAIKU

Into the tunnel
last glance at England
the Burger King sign

On the stationary coach
the huddle of poets
moves forward at speed

Crossing the channel
praying to see
not one drop of water

Beneath water and rock
the poets' hearts beat
in metrical stress

We pass without knowing
the navvy's lost ring
buried in rock

*Written on National Poetry Day, 1997, on an invited trip
through the tunnel with 30 members of The British Haiku
Society.*

TWENTY SEVEN HAIKU

*From the author's book, Broke Through Britain, a 540
mile penniless journey from Plymouth to Edinburgh,
where each day's writing began with a relevant haiku.*

1
Far from home
my son's biroed name
fades from my skin

2
Quick into the prison
then out again
the innocent sparrows

3
In the Dartmoor rain
the lonely hitch-hiker
sees cars brake for sheep

4
The cider-maker's
glass eye
has seen it all

5
Yanked towards heaven
the peaceful bell-ringers
are dropped back to earth

6
Wearing Levannah's necklace
while she bathes
my dog

7
All day on the settee
doing nothing
my journey advances

8
The two women
I just met
stroking my naked feet

9
Fed with his wife's ashes
the rowan tree
flowers brilliant red

10
Walking all day
at evening I drink
from the same river

11
Fresh eggs on toast
in the doorway
the watching hens

12
Heatwave at last
carefully John removes
the cow's skin

13
On the neatly trimmed lawn
the neatly curled
dog turd

14
Too hot to dance
except for the cows
caught in the heat haze

15
After walking twenty miles
I enjoy the fly's journey
on my cooling feet

16
The grey lake
calls to the grey sky
which will soon respond

17
In the sluggish canal
the new haiku
refuses to move

18
Pursuing the horizon ahead
behind us another one
keeps pace

19
On the pavilion board
easily reached
a record score

20
Staying close to my heel
nothing now
but my shadow

21
Through the forest trees
the sun moves with me
rests when I rest

22
On the moorland top
the snow poles trembling
in the August wind

23
At the wood's edge
the final tree
is also the first tree

24
High on the moorland
only the wind
and the sucking of my sweet

25
Round the historic ruin
two generations of sheep
chew into the future

26
Rain hits my brolly
slides to earth
further north than me

27
The final day
not even the sun
can beat me home

WHAT WILL WE TELL THEM?

What will we tell them
when their song birds won't sing
and their dreams have been drowned in a sack
and their lollipop sticks are washed down the drain
and the sunshine is not coming back?

What will we tell them
when the doll's in the bin
and their toys gather dust on the floor
and their nursery rhymes are a scream in the dark
and we tuck in their blankets no more?

What will we tell them
when they leave the school yard
and their text-books are taken away
and we cast them adrift on a grey groaning tide
washing in, washing out, every day?

What will we tell them
when we ask them to kill
for some reason they did not create
and we give them their guns
and we wave them away
while the brass band plays at the gate?

What will we tell them
when it's all come to nought
and they visit our graves twice a year
and their children toss flowers
where no flowers can grow
which then shrivel, are blown, disappear?

FRONT ROOM

A Welsh dresser, heavy oak table
sweetly polished by Johnstons.
Blocking the cold fireplace
a screen of embroidered pastel.
In the hearth, a copper shovel
tongues and brush
motionless on their tree.

A room not often used.

Twice a month, mother took down
the brasses, tore pungent pink wadding
from a tin, its blush
blackening at first rub.
Once a week she dusted ornaments
then returned them to obscurity.
The stiff-backed chairs at the table
stood smartly to attention.
Crammed under the piano stool lid
a generation of sheet music
none of us could read.

Sunday dinner was served in that room.
And Christmas tea — a gathering
of distant family who slurped peaches
and Carnation. We didn't understand
their warts, their medical complaints
their bitter tales of divorce
their illfitting suits.

Normally the room was empty
as if something was preserved
something not everyday
a sense of hushed removal.
In the Welsh dresser were drawers
of never used table mats
heavy cutlery lying in state
crockery stacked for a special occasion
white cloths, ironed stiff
and unseen. In that silence
our tread shook slightly
the propped willow pattern plates.

Sometimes we were summoned to that room.
A stern father laid us across his knee
the cane's thin thwack leaving our skin
like hot coals. As we moved
choking, out the kitchen door
mother would busy herself
wrists-deep in suds, clanking pots
through her tight silence.

LOG

Sunk into firm sand
dug deep in its own grave
only the rounded spine visible.
Each tide pressed it further
into the beach's clenched fist.
Soon it would be gone.
Not missing, like a child is missing
like a pet goes astray, just gone.

My son Dylan kicked its immovable mass.
'Lets dig it out" he said.
"Impossible" I replied and we moved on.
At midnight he persuaded our return
three of us, the black sea sky
streaked with a solitary gull
no noise but the hiss of clapped-out waves.
Dylan and Brian dug with bare hands
like those frantic searchers
for earthquake survivors. The crater
stretched wider. Slowly log spread its dark mass.
Four feet long, as thick as an elephant's leg
each end cut smooth for a purpose we didn't know.
They dug deep down, to where soaked sand
held the sea in some cold secret.
I heaved log from its wet bed;
a sucking sound. Noticed at its middle
a sawn off leprous stump which would make
rolling impossible. I stood it on end
tottering like a drunk, dropped it forward
with a thick thud. On end again
and dropped again, turning its slow journey
like some lazy acrobat. And each turn
of its heavy silent mass left me deep breathing.
Heaved and heaved to the beach top, beyond the reach
of the fingering tide; Dylan and Brian
scampering like excited dogs.

We left it that night under the slipway wall
part of its own shadow. And returned
next morning with clattering trolley.
Lugged and heaved log again, laid it down
like some anaesthetised patient
trundled it up the steep slope
the small trolley wheels creaking at its weight
one hand holding it steady
as if on a fevered brow.

In the back yard we stood it again
brushed the clinging sand from its soaked surface
waltzed it in in four-two time through the kitchen door
propped it against the old black range.
It leaned like some casual visitor
soon to light a fag, or doff his hat.
Its weight rucked up the mat
indented the fire surround paint.

What purpose did it once have?
How long in that sea?
How long burrowing in that sand?

Before sleeping that night
I looked in at Dylan's tousled head
looked in at log's pock-marked bulk.
The fire's dying embers
pushed it further into shadow.

For six weeks it dried. Nothing would hurry it.
The world fought itself, dragged itself from bed
made plans, journeyed blind.
No necessity quickened log, no shouting
no sweet murmuring. Slowly its complexion changed.
Its dark stain paled to domestic beige.
Its damp surface toughened and cracked.
Every third day we turned it
reversed the gravity of its drying.
Bit by bit log expelled that sea
which had sucked it like a lozenge.

Bone-dry, I lay it by the fire;
a piece of furniture, some thing of use.
Visitors sat on it, stood on it
wobbling like circus clowns.

Seasons darkened. At times with the night house
too quiet to breathe, I would lay on log
become part of its tempered bulk
and know, that like me
it had no reason for leaving.

And Dylan ran free, ran further, for longer
log drifting into the blur of young history
the midnight crater long since washed flat
by forgotten tides.

And still I heave log on end
Still totter it like a drunk
not wanting that sometime day
when log will refuse to be heaved.

SEEING TO THE UNMADE FIRE

I cannot look long on the unmade fire
its cold ashes, its dark unbeating heart
its clinker as brittle as honeycomb.
I need to poke and rake, to riddle down
its spent husks, need to brush and pan
into plastic bags its lifeless grey.
And from the empty grate, begin again.

First its base of scrunched and ragged
paper clouds; then more newspaper
twizzled tight into curled sticks.
Then kindling, criss-crossed, latticed slopes
on which the weighted coal slightly gives.

I can leave it then.
All day the chimney will suck it
like an unlit fag
but I can leave it.

ONE DOZEN BEST SELLING BOOKS I AM PREPARING TO WRITE

Loud Nuns
Blinking for Beginners
The Final Doughnut
Dogs Talk about Horses
My Life in Tin
False Leg Syndrome
Shepshed or Bust
Hair Care After Death
Porridge Maintenance
The History of Whistling Abroad
When to Cough
Fudge Hell

CEMETERY *(ONE)*

We stay silent from respect
bow our heads, bend our knee
to lay quiet flowers. Our children
are shushed at our side.
Laughter is turned back
at the heavy iron gate.

As if the dead
did not hear enough silence.
As if the dead
would find fault with laughter.
Trussed in their Sunday best
their mouths pressed shut
their veins chemically filled
their rouge long faded
with their buried dreams
of a distant sky.

Wake them up;
with a big drum
with fireworks
singers in the trees
brightly twirled ribbons
acrobats at the gravestone
a procession, dancing its noisy way
past the line of black cars
kept always in bottom gear.

CEMETERY *(TWO)*

How the lines
of gravestones spread.
The unstoppable progress
of the dead.

HOW, WHO, WHAT, WHY & WHEN?

How come God doesn't dance?
Who's ever heard God singing?
What's God's laughter sound like?
Why this big deal about God
When he doesn't even dance?

TORN APART

For three days the wind
has shrieked itself hoarse
has torn the leaves
from their deep love of the tree.

Soon those leaves will
dance and swirl
along the chilling street.
Brown, brittle dead.

And the tree will shiver
in its skeleton, dig deep
into its roots and sing
its silent song of spring.

JUST KEEPS DOING IT

1.
The sea is teasing the beach
like a hand on an inner thigh:
it's nosing its slow curiosity
round the back of forgotten rocks
carrying in its wet palm
the discarded Embassy pack

Just keeps doing it

2.
The sea is swelling its hunched strength
it may crash down a thudded fist
or pour over the harbour wall
like the front-runners at Beechers*

Just keeps doing it

3.
The sea is the scherzo conductor
flashing and flailing his arms
the sea is the Eastern mystic
lying prone for days

Just keeps doing it

Listen. Drowned sailors are calling
summoning us to that shoreline
where the sea just keeps doing it
all the time

*Beechers Brook — famous Grand National jump

THE IMPORTANT THING

The important thing
is not fashion
but what you do
not what changes
but the change in you

Be unambitious
if the ambitious demand
even bigger desks
Be impractical
if the practical dream only
of drip-free emulsion

Invite failure out
for the occasional drink
Enjoy the restaurant
when your table is laid
for just one

And when a child studies hard
a simple piece of wood
study the wood too
though your eyesight
is slowly worsening

POEMLETS

WORTH KNOWING
Ardor
can make things
harder

NON-GOVERNMENT HEALTH WARNING
Too much sex
is good for you

A POEM IMPOSSIBLE TO PRONOUNCE CORRECTLY
Alfa Romeo
and Juliet

NECESSARY PROCEDURE
Censorship
must be censored

DEFINITION
Mortal — *Drunk*
Immortal — *Drunk for ever and ever*

PAVEMENT ARTIST
Last night's biriani
picked clean by
the spring-heeled sparrows
of morning

AT LAST
Good morning
Godot!

GONE

He is not warmed by the sun
The wind does not chill him now
What fears wake him in the night?
None. What does he dream?
Nothing. He is gone

Leave his heavy coat on its hook
the folded shirts in the drawer
No need yet to clear the shed
put back his favourite book

Someone else will sit in that chair
The footsteps on the stair not his
That shadow at the window — a stranger's
Whose laugh in the hall? Another's

Look out into your garden
A crow is rising in flight
The large wings that will lift it to freedom
must first blot out the sun.

I WANT TO DIE AND BE THOUGHT GOOD OF

I want to die and be thought good of
I want people who walk behind my coffin
to wonder who gets my purple socks
I want those who look at my photo to laugh
at the soup stain on the jacket
I want the date I died to be remembered
by squidgy chocolate cake
eaten by people who simultaneously
roar with laughter and bubble up
I want someone to pick up a book of mine
and be inspired to paint the gate
I want them to look at my son
and for a short time be preoccupied
with the length of my nose
I want them to wake in the stillness of night
exclaim, "Shit! He's dead!"
then return to uninterrupted slumber
I want them to come across some small object of mine
a ring maybe, or necklace
and think, "I'll have that!"
I want the odd person to miss me so much
they're arrested for digging me up
and given a suspended sentence
I want the occasional argument
about how long I had a beard
I want unconfirmed sightings
of me riding waves off Cullercoats beach
I want that long leather coat (the fantasy rock star one)
to be left hanging on its hook
for an indeterminate time
for however long it takes.

THIS POEM IS NOT SPONSORED

This poem is not sponsored by:
Barclays Bank, Northern Electric, Budweiser Beer,
Trust House Forte, McDonalds, Reed International,
English Estates, Scottish & Newcastle or Snicker Bars

This poem does not acknowledge the assistance of:
Chase Manhattan, Carling Black Label, British Airways,
Natwest, BNFL, Kleinwort Benson, Texas Homecare,
Tonka Toys, McAlpine, British American Tobacco,
ICI, Scottish Widows, IBM, Balfour Beatty, Woolco,
Tate & Lyle or Nissan Cars

This poem's creation was not made possible by:
United Biscuits, Black & Decker, Currys Electric,
British Telecom, Heineken, Kwik-Fit Exhausts, Virgin
Atlantic, Coca Cola, Legal & General, Amstrad,
W.H.Smith, Storey Carpets, Cable & Wireless, Burger
King, Dulux Paint or Raleigh Bikes

Future poetry sponsorship is not actively sought from:
Pearl Assurance, Tetley Breweries, British Steel,
Nintendo, Gillette, Panasonic, Adidas, The Prudential,
Procter & Gamble, Barratt Homes, Safeway, Bradford
& Bingley, Tupperware or Spud-U-Like.

CORRECTIONS & CLARIFICATIONS

In the article on the transcendentalist Mishu Tikky Zat (Sept 3), Zat was quoted as saying, "Let there be no doubt of this — anyone can jump from a 17th storey window in complete safety." This should have read: "Let there be no doubt of this — no-one can jump from a 17th storey window in complete safety."

In the review of the new Hart Willow novel, *Spaghetti*(Aug 31), the sentence "this could prove to be the deftest writing of the century" should have read, "this could prove to be the daftest writing of the century."

Our report on the Spurs v Everton game (Sept. 2) contained the sentence, "In the 31st minute, Edwards made a fantastic save from a typical Lawrenson piledriver". The intended sentence was "the entire stadium collapsed in an earthquake engulfing all 31,000 spectators."

In the interview with the Czech sculptor Yannek Nek (Sept 1), the artist was quoted as saying: "My work is a cry for humanity past present and future, a dark scream from the pitiless depths to which civilisation has sunk". The sculptor's agent has asked us to point out the correct quotation is "My next commission is from Coca-Cola, to build a 50ft high Coke bottle outside their global headquarters."

In the news story on the collapsing Shropshire bridge disaster (Aug 30), which claimed 328 lives, including those of 187 schoolchildren, the county's chief structural engineer was referred to as Mr. George H.H. Meekin. We have been asked to point out the correct nomenclature is Mr. George H.H.H. Meekin.

The obituary notice on the American film star, Kirk 'Fast Lane' Farringdon, had one contemporary quoted as saying, "Fast Lane had the biggest dick in Hollywood." This should have read "Fast Lane was the biggest dick in Hollywood."

THE DOCTOR ASKS DIFFERENT PEOPLE
TO SAY "AAAH!"

(An audience participation poem. The audience is encouraged to interpret the word "aaah!" in the most imaginative way possible, as they think it would fit each name).

The man in the moon
Ghenghis Khan's mother-in-law
The man at the minor road works operating STOP/GO
Adolf Hitler's parrot
The back four of Leyton Orient FC reserves
An underwater snorkler
A person being tortured with red-hot knives
A beekeeper pursued by an entire swarm
Rupert Murdoch's goldfish
The Queen preparing to open parliament
Albert Einstein in a thick balaclava
Marcel Marceau
The Poet Laureate after a large bowl of pasta
The audience present here today

GUEST SPEAKER

The chairman tinks his glass;
introduces the guest speaker.
"A man who needs no introduction...
his long association with the game."

Applause ripples the speaker to his feet.
The after-dinner air is acrid with cigars
the stiff white table cloths freckled with soup.
A few men swirl their brandy glasses
to miniature tsunamis.

He's a pro. Speaks from memory
starts with a joke (one of the lads).
That one about scoring mid-week
(it always goes down well).
The audience has slugged pints in the bar
Chardonnay with the salmon *en croute*
the steak *au poivre*, the arctic roll.
By evening's end they'll be spread wide
like Humpty Dumpties. They like tit-bits
gossip; that England striker and the newscaster
that manager and the chairman's wife.
Is that Chelsea striker really a poofter?

He gives them enough to chew on
enough to earn his three ton. He knows that's small beer
compared to the Fergies, the Wengers. The asking price
tumbles when the cameras have gone elsewhere.
Some remember his playing days
that 30 yarder against Leeds in '58
the three-times taken penalty against Spurs
the famous Bolton semi-final.
But mainly it's Big Des, the seven club manager
the wide hats, the shocking ties, the outrageous
programme notes, the dug-out antics
the clashes with the board, the posing
with *The Sun* Page Three.

He speaks for 25 minutes. Time for questions.
He's heard them all. Could do it in his sleep.
Does he miss the involvement since retirement?
What — with 18 holes on his doorstep!
What does he think of the present premiership?
Mostly, he'd rather not.
And missing that title on goal difference?
Shit happens.

The chairman rises to thank him.
"I'm sure we'd all like to show–"
The heartily thumped tables
slightly shimmy the chandelier
and tremble the tank-heavy cutlery.

In the bar he's open to autographs
side-steps the haulage contractor
who thinks the game has too many wogs.
He taxis home in the dark
(some drivers still recognise him).
The cream sauce squats in his stomach.
En route he checks future fixtures
Hartlepool Chamber of Trade
Burnley Rotary, Double Glazing Convention.
Bookings slightly down.
But then the game's not what it was.
That was the way things went.
That's what he'd tell Sheila
as she lay Mogadonned in bed.
Take each booking as it came.
It was a funny old game.
One minute over the moon
the next —

SECRETS OF SUCCESS

Eat garlic prior to a dental visit
practice flatulence in a crowded lift
remark immediately on friends' increased weight
talk persistently to graveside mourners
invite past partners on your honeymoon
keep souvenir vomit in a coffee table jar
frame your dead lover's toe
persuade your suicidal friends to go ahead
boo at RSC premieres
attend all interviews drunk and two days late
snore during sex
brush your hair above the delicatessen counter
answer the telephone without speaking
in meditation class, read aloud this poem.

Also Available from Five Leaves

Passionate Renewal: Jewish poetry in Britain since 1945. An anthology edited by *Peter Lawson*
354 pages, 0 907123 73 2, £14.99
A Poetry Book Society Special Commendation

Dannie Abse **Richard Burns** Ruth Fainlight **Elaine Feinstein** Karen Gershon **Michael Hamburger** Philip Hobsbaum **Michael Horovitz** A.C. Jacobs **Bernard Kops** Lotte Kramer **Joanne Limburg** Emanuel Litvinoff **Gerda Mayer** Jeremy Robson **Michael Rosen** Jon Silkin **George Szirtes** Jonathan Treitel **Daniel Weissbort**

The act of gathering these (poets) together reveals the importance of Jewish writers to a wider British tradition, both as poets, but also as translators, and communicators with the wider world. This is an important and revealing anthology.
POETRY BOOK SOCIETY

The Art of Blessing the Day: Poems on Jewish Themes by *Marge Piercy*
0 907123 47 3, 200 pages, £7.99
A collection based on themes of family (*mishpocheh*), repair of the world (*tikkun olam*), history and interpretation (*toladot, midrashim*), prayer (*tefillah*) and the Jewish year (*ha-shana*).

This is what I want from poetry: generosity, sensuous imagery, musicality, celebration, the voice of community.
POETRY QUARTERLY REVIEW

Gardens of Eden Revisited by *Michelene Wandor*
0 907123 62 7, 186 pages, £7.99
...a gossipy irresistible send-up of the Old Testament. VOGUE

The Radical Twenties: Writing, Politics, Culture by *John Lucas*
0 907123 17 1, 263 pages, £11.99
What is particularly valuable in this book is the attention Lucas gives to a number of texts from the 1920s that have had less attention than they deserve in literary-critical accounts of the decade... the dust-jacket photograph of Nan Youngman in 1925 with cigarette and guitar, so wonderfully evocative of the spirit Lucas respects and consistently carries forward in his writing.
MLR

This is No Book: A Gay Reader by *Gregory Woods*
0 907123 26 0, 112 pages, £6.95
...a marvellous read - witty and independent and full of shrewd insights from, I suppose, the foremost gay poet working in Britain today. If you want to map out a gay canon, start here: a colleague asked me what had been done on gay poetics and I can't think of anything better. GAY TIMES

Poems for the Beekeeper edited by *Robert Gent*
0 907123 82 1, 176 pages, £6.99
Dannie Abse **Fleur Adcock** James Berry **Alan Brownjohn** Catheryn Byron **Wendy Cope** Robert Creeley **Kwame Dawes** Carol Anne Duffy **Helen Dunmore** Gavin Ewart **UA Fanthorpe** Elaine Feinstein **John Harvey** Adrian Henri **Selima Hill** Mick Imlah **Jenny Joseph** Jackie Kay **Liz Lochhead** Michael Longley **John Lucas** Roger McGough **Ian McMillan** Wes Magee **Adrian Mitchell** Henry Normal **Brian Patten** Tom Paulin **Nigel Planer** Peter Porter **Peter Redgrove** Christopher Reid **Vernon Scannell** Penelope Shuttle **Jon Silkin** Ken Smith and **Charles Tomlinson** are represented by up to four poems each in this collection celebrating 15 years of the Beeston Poets readings.

Laughing All the Way by *Liz Cashdan*
0 907123 46 5, 70 pages, £5.99
Includes the acclaimed Tyre-Cairo letters — a dramatic reconstruction of an 11th century Jewish family, which won the *Jewish Quarterly* Wingate Prize.

The Smug Bridegroom by *Robert Hamberger*
0 907123 88 0, 78 pages, £6.99
A set of deeply personal poems, reconciling the anecdotal and the rhetorical. His writing traces the shifts in family life, break up and renewal.
Robert Hamberger writes in a deceptively simple manner. A must for poetry readers and a perfect introduction for the curious.
GAY TIMES
I've often seen the sonnet as a kind of straightjacket in the wrong hands, but Hamberger makes them fly. IAN MCMILLAN

Five Leaves' books are available from bookshops or, post free, from Five Leaves, PO Box 81, Nottingham NG5 4ER. A full catalogue is available on www.fiveleaves.co.uk.